The Willow Howl
Lisa Brognano

Nixes Mate Books
Allston, Massachusetts

Copyright © 2017 Lisa Brognano

Book design by d'Entremont
Cover photo from the collection of Lauren Leja

All rights reserved. This book or any portion thereof may not be reproduced or used in any manner whatsoever without the express written permission of the publisher except for the use of brief quotations in a book review or scholarly journal.

Special thanks to my mother for her proofreading genius, my father for reading my poems when they appear in magazines, my sister, Maria, and nephews Tyler and Noah for their enjoyment of my work, and especially to my husband, James, for his endless support of my writing. An enormous thank you to Michael McInnis for being terrific and everyone at Nixes Mate. Most importantly, I thank God and Mary.

ISBN 978-0-9991882-3-1

Nixes Mate Books
POBox 1179
Allston, MA 02134
nixesmate.pub/books

For my sister, Josie, love always and forever

Contents

Willow Howl	1
Carpet Of Stars	3
Hearth Rug	4
Snow And Grown Men	5
As One	6
Foot Of The Statue	7
Time's	8
Ode To Down Below	9
First Date	10
Hailing A Taxi	11
Shook Off	12
A & B	14
Come Here	15
Six-Year-Old	16
Field	17
The Primordial Watch	18
Retired	19
Rite Of Passage	20
Cross The Wood So	21
After Rain	22
Jed	23
Summer Drought	24
Solid Wall	25
Middle Of The Night	26

Car	27
Part Of Her	28
Poor	29
Chasm	30
Weary Weak	31
Bay Window	32
Storm	33
Leo	34
Day Wage	35
Festival	36
Solomon Fred	38
A Vase Of Roses	39
Child's Game	40
Golden Barrette	41
Aged	42
Old Elaine	43
Suntanned Laborers	44
The Descent	45
Pelt And Crumble	46
Sly Boys Gliding	47
Struggling Stardom	48
Plain Truth	49
A Stroll In The Dark	50
Blizzard Then	52
Sun-Blotted Plainswoman	53

The Willow Howl

Willow Howl

Driving past a winter of trees,
        dry wool earth by the edge of the

Road, fine fold of trees, flock

Of oak and glorious dead wood,
        every one gray . . . herd of willows.

But it is the overwhelming flesh of the
        sky, such gray vague

Held over the cold crunch of bare things,

But exaggerate one tree and you've
        reached the sky

Where the wind lives peacefully like
        many, many silk shawls on snow.

Fierce confusing wind is nothing more
        than a hollow gesture to torture

The stiff branch, yet they bend and throw
     themselves curling just to organize
          better what the wind does.

That lump of wind.

Driving past a winter of trees the willow
     howls, the sky turns shallow and

Swallows itself, leaving the inside flap of
     Heaven ajar, from which floats down
          a wise owl and others like it.

Carpet Of Stars

I dreamt of deer tracks.
I woke up panting.
I washed my neck and went
Walking diagonally through
A carpet of stars – snow on the
Ground – toward a clump of men
And women waiting for the hum
Of a bus – we all worked the night shift.

I looked over my shoulders at our scuffy
Dotty marks to get here, scuffy dotty marks.
I leaned and patted the others having no
Purpose but to warm my hands on the necks
Of their furry coats.

Hearth Rug

Intricate flame of candle
                rises firmly in the glow of

Drip-shape, yellow-dot, burn-luck,
                the night is fine, flexible

Like the meal, the man, the lady
                crossing her legs on the sofa,

The way they move closer – sound of
                raindrops on the patio roof, as if

Rain could flicker, it sounded that way,
                calm, smooth, and daring.

Snow And Grown Men

Falling
Snow is like the white dots
On dice, shook off, rolled fat
For throwing at third-story windows.

Grown men get hit on their backs by
Boys who run and hide, wet glad.

Grown men swear and shovel, vow
Never to spawn brats, swear, shovel
Go cross-eyed, take the coffee their wives
Bring out, kiss her, keep shoveling.

As One

He clutched my fingertips
                and we understood

The deaf part of our love,
                such giant faint gain.

We agreed to hide ourselves
                inside the shapes of

Our bodies, the tonsil cup
                of stuffed love, the
                              zigzag of tender tongues.

The fluff of sinking into something, that
                rising apart from something,
                              that space between

two things.

Foot Of The Statue

You have switched and are now cold
You have folded our love in half and
Creased it many times I gazed at you
Sighting your sorrow like a hallow
A brimful of burden do not set out to
Boggle me just leave me quietly I need
To juggle with my wall of thickened love
Yet I watch strangers in the park picking
Flowers putting daisies at the foot of the statue.

Time's

Time's a twig picked up by an animal
And carted deeper into the woods.

Time sprouts, grows into a tree.
Time is cut down.
Time's a seed.
Time flies over a field.

Time's a twig...time's carted;
Time's a tree...time's cut down.

Ode To Down Below

Birds slap into the sky dense
Shrugged up into blue fade on blue
They are watched and shot.

Generally songbirds moan.
Big broad moans echo into
Vast high hollow.

Brown birds borrow their sorrow
While they bicker, soar and stagger.

Generally, a mountain crevasse is
A blessing, a sweet sort of refuge
A place to die, beauty burial, aerial
View of multitude of treetops, oh
Soothing deathbed, oh high bench,
Oh shooter down below.

First Date

So much depended on that eager
Moment, that outdoor moonshine time.

A picnic basket held limes
And wine and the thickest Florida
Prime rib. No pie, no cake.

The man and lady were shaking
Cutely like kettles, touching their
Elbows, tilting their heads.

They were gentle people with calm
Ideas, lovers of shooting stars.

The red wine, the green limes, the
Noises of the night echoing like gongs
On trees, gongs on trees, gongs on trees.

Hailing A Taxi

She wore many bracelets, each
Was a noodle on her wrist, she
Wore a shirt with a pocket and
It had lovely designs on it, quite
Odd for an executive, a pacifist,
Tall anti-war girl, a woman dis-
Tressed with global warming.
The corridors echoed with the
Ping of her heels as she said bye,
Bye, take care, to the mealy-
Mouthed man and walked out
Of the building, hailing a taxi,
The driver puffed his smoke out
The rolled-down window, saying
He didn't care much for heavy
Snowy winters, much less driving
Through slush.

Shook Off

Dog   wants
        his   fur   free

Of flies
        And   small beetles.

Needs his
        castle clean.

        Roam in
            comfort, follow

A man,
        Be   an   animal. He

Wants
        adventure
and   follows

Closely…

                    Even if hours go by,

A dog
          will always
               walk at a man's

Pace.

A & B

Sound comes from a button-like boom;
Earth comes from a chamber-tucked lump;
Sight comes from a quick circle whirling;
Touch comes from fine flannel nooks;
Smell is neutral, coming from last year's
Prize-winning rainwater.

Come Here

Why don't you care if the house falls
on us?

Why is it my responsibility to wedge this house
for us?

Do you think I have tricks in a bag to pull out and
save us?

Keep sitting there leaning back forgetting
about us.

I don't offer you coffee anymore because it ain't
our glue, not us, not a black stiff drink.

Do what I ask, Dan, do come here.

Come over here and take off your coat and lay it
over us.

Six-Year-Old

"She won't be coming back, dear."
"Why won't she?"
"She took ill, dear, you recall?"
"Yeah, I sawed it."
"Well then, dear boy, you ought to know
                      she ain't be back no more."
"On account of my lying?"
"No on account of her own dying."
"Why'd she have to go and do it, then?"
"She done what her sore poor body gone
                      and made her do."

Field

As a Harvester, you gather
My thoughts keenly, and
When my tools of field grow tattered

Your sickle swings gentle and deft – rather
Than cut, it cleanses the land.
As a Harvester, you gather

The peas – podded and parented; rather
A linear family – bedded by the soil and sand.
When my tools of field grow tattered

My leafy skin loosens; a muddy lather
Tills my veins, a furrow fruitless and bland.
As a Harvester, you gather

Corn in all its yellow matter, as so
Many ears of corn upon the land.
When my tools of field grow tattered

My beet eyes know only to gather
Rain – the hoe and tiller await your plan,
As a Harvester, you gather
When my tools of field grow tattered.

The Primordial Watch

I inquired: "Cave man, what time is it?"
He wound up his club ... and struck my watch. Three
Stones from the cave's ledge fell into a pit.

I told him not to worry his wit,
But I must count the time passed under this tree.
I inquired: "Cave man, what time is it?"

When he punches his time card to quit
Work at the Bow and Arrow Shop, then he will see.
Stones from the cave's ledge fell into a pit,

Only two descended this time. Both split
And shattered – like my watch, unnecessarily.
I inquired: "Cave man, what time is it?"

Perhaps midnight, as that counterfeit
Clock, the moon, looms above so predictably.
Stones from the cave's ledge fell into a pit,

Though solely one this time: no compatriots
To break the fall or end the monotony ...
I inquired: "Cave man, what time is it?"
Stones from the cave's ledge fell into a pit.

Retired

Work brought you through life
To an old man, it kept you busy
But now it has dropped you flat,
Like the easy part of a sit up, and
You're fatter too, as if all those
Paychecks stuffed you.

You lay on a lawn chair,
Barely golfing, fawning over
Dusty books on carpentry, worn.
One day you imagine trying adultery,
But your wife makes good, sweet tea so
You could never cheat, the sag in your
Shoulders is bound to increase.

Rite Of Passage

A child hid a stone but found
A sunnier prettier small rock
And figured a flimsy rock would
Hide better than a stone so he
Shimmed a tree, out to the limb.

Mama would be livid, if she found out.
Would swear colorfully, if she found out.
Would holler and collar him, if she found out.

Immediately,
>> She'd murder
>>>> That fruit tree.

Rufus had climbed up and looked
Over the fence, for the first time.

Cross The Wood So

Generous clear flow, wooden watering pail;
Deep purple flowers drink. Tweedle-twaddle,
Water drips across old Patty's homemade lattice.

Neighbors say it takes an authentic rustic trusting
Man to cross the skinny wood so – after all it is
Coon River Junction.

Patty makes lattice because he's so good at it and
He's got nothing else to do but cross the wood so.

After Rain

Weather looks smeared today,
           Spread-thin clouds, gray-beige
                    Light, trees hazy but houses

Crisp. Rain blurs everything
           As it pours down
                    Until it stops, clear, crisp

New kind of world. The pavement
           Appears to be black silk.

Jed

Shy the same as Pa.
Quick to learn like Ma.

Lanky as Pa.
Broadhanded like Ma.

Able to fish. Partly
Able to sew socks.

Good in school; capable
Of catching catfish.

Follows current events;
Wonders why
quilts are hung on walls.

Summer Drought

The heated days are blank with
The fervor of sweat and stark
Sunshine. Dry lawns edge forward
In brown blades but the rains don't
Come.

Every aspect of the shrill land cries
Out but it is a useless endeavor. The
Thirsty earth takes second place to
Another plan. There is no involvement
With the pouring, wet, refreshing rains
That shot down from the sky last summer.

This summer is different – moody and
Vengeful. Such dryness makes it homely.
On and on the dry days stretch and crack in
A bantering melody. Thin and bitter, the days
Miss their allotment of Nature's fruits.

A sadness brims and echoes. Why doesn't the
Rain come? Why doesn't it bother with the
Simple soil?

Solid Wall

Walls rarely bend, never
Trim themselves and cannot
Goad you, adore you, restore
Your sense of thick mass,
Bold, the walls balance the
Roof.

Great fear we have of
Walls, bold, nice to know
There are doors to go out
And come in, not just
Walls but solid men
Who adore you.

Do not make the same
Mistake as the ceiling
Which spread out over
Its legs, the walls, like
The body of a spider,
The roof. The house is
Filled with girls made by
The man and woman, the
Walls are very solid.

Middle Of The Night

Climbing through the window
                made the boy lurch onto the

Girl's bed. She tickled him as
                he came at her, how slow and

Thoughtfully they kissed.

Car

I'm learning a lot about what it means
To be whole, carefree, and own a car.

The things I learn are full of tenderness,
Clearly life, but the things I let slip by are
Bold about it. They creep and fling, wiggle
And shudder, bounce and swallow. They
Come at me until I learn them.

I am not street smart, so I look away. Life
Calls me a chicken – chicken going down the
Highway.

Part Of Her

She fell into the groove of life
And out of the groove came the
Children and the husband and the
Housework. Part of her tilted to do
The chores and part of her found new
Grooves under the dark wooden table.

Her parents had been hard-workers.
Her grandparents had been hard-workers.
It was passed down.
The grooves would always be there.

Poor

Small iron lamp,
Midsized table,
Two children idle
In the doorway, soup
On the table and milk
In fat cups.

Chasm

He yells to her over
Big bank of hills and
Sees nothing but blunt
Brown banks and a snake
River below.

She hears Tom and from
Her ledge moves a little,
Sees the river and some grass.

He strains and pivots, parting
The grass. She remains still
And pale, swallows some air,
As she sees him climb over
The flow of the river where
The rocks lay. He won't stay
Long, he has to get back.

Weary Weak

A straight lump under covers,
Light pink and hot pink blanket,
Shivering, whining, long day,
Needs the kind of rest that comes
From living simply – little lump of
Soul sugar – overworked mama
Is stretched thin and flat out. Her
Arms quiver from all the broom-handling,
Swept and mopped the wooden floors until
The front entry lacked the footprints.

Same sort of thing will happen tomorrow
If the weary weak woman crawls out of bed.

Bay Window

Trees sway to mimic the wind –
maples and oaks mingle –
as if they'd gotten knotted;
Potted plants lack the same sort of exercise
But stoic sycamores sway, heydaying,
Delirious in the sunlight.

Shimmering light slants through
The windowpanes –

Our potted plant
Sits on the ledge
Of a bay window.

Storm

Get the boat
and let's leave,
drag over the
oars quick,
pull back
the tarp
and snap
down the seats,
we've got no time
to dally or bet or beg –
coaxing
the waving wind
and the slapping sea
is futile.

Tomorrow will
Seem brighter.

Leo

Leo's feet dangled, he sat on the table,
His eyes hopped around the room,
Most of the room was empty, the chair
Near the fireplace had a bluish-purple
Quilt on it with stars, moons, crosses.

His mother would bring hamburgers for
Dinner and he would drink all his milk.
She would demand he hop down from the
Table and behave like a good boy with
Manners, how she raised him to be polite.

Didn't matter much to Leo. Slumping
His shoulders made the meat go down
Easy and later in the evening he would
Dream about tomorrow's meal. But not
Always. Sometimes he imagined a shiny
bicycle appearing on the sidewalk.

Day Wage

Brass and iron
plus rod-ready supplies
burst into the factory
from an import.
The manager jots his name on a form and yells:
the brass looks fine,
the iron rusty,
the steel corroded.

How much do we owe?

Delivery man nods and points to an amount
on the page; scratches his jaw until the owner
grumbles and trots off to a nearby office.

Business is slow and the factory stinks
of welding fumes
And grease streaks the floors.

But the brass looks fine,
the iron rusty,
the steel corroded.

Festival

Tubs filled with apples piled high
Cram the boulevard and cars
Pull over and crawl while wives
Reach their arms selecting fruit –
The Seasonal Festival

Crows are let go into the
Sky for luck, luck and leisure.

Only farmer's wives would try
An odd modern way, such a
Drive-by way, apples in tubs,
Arms out windows, cars with fruit,
Bumper to bumper farm trucks.

Crows are let go into the
Sky for luck, luck and leisure.

If anyone leaves his car
Attempting to go on foot
They are reminded to drive
By, enjoy the ride, mister,
That's how we do things 'round here.

Crows are let go into the
Sky for luck, luck and leisure.

Solomon Fred

A swarm of true love
Came over the boy and girl.
A valuable parade was held
In their honor, floats with
Flowers and fruit.

He was firmly homely
But tall and dark
And she swept him up
Like forest-brown acorns,
And she called him
Solomon Fred.

Entire town wished them
Well, fat farmable faith
Sung songs of bliss, bless
Blah and so on. The parade
Rolled up the street.

A Vase Of Roses

Sits on my counter and people say,
"Oh, how lovely!" They are the same flowers
from the bush outside my lime-green door,
By the front steps, they squat silently, unnoticed,
a part of the scenery.

When I cut them, stem for stem, and plop them in a
vase…people bend their necks to sniff the roses.

It happens all summer long. The lovely roses are
sniffed on my countertop. A fragrance like butterflies
coasting over the bay of the Atlantic. They are
noticed for their beauty in my bright yellow kitchen.

Drifting and soaring, a fragrance like butterflies
coasting over the bay
of the Atlantic,
the soft scent of
pale pink roses,
fully open,
petals falling
into the waves,
mingling with seaweed,
resembling shells.

Child's Game

Rolling a coin across
The tile floor, going to
The place where it stopped.
Rolling it again and going
To the place.

Rolling
           a
                      coin

across
           the
                  tile
                          floor.

Golden Barrette

The queen wears her hair
up but refuses the golden
barrette –

She jumps on a horse,
a colicky beast that only
obeys her.

The brown mare gallops
through golden sun –
Blue hills and tan fields
toward another castle.

The home of Jerome,
a duke, a quiet ruler,
a tall man, an aggravated
farmer himself, since the
drought – his dizzy head,
his moans for the queen
have brought her near.

And it is her desire to
mend him.

Aged

Dragged down by the young,
I am old.
Told over and over,
I am old.
Grown into what I am,
Old.

Thousands of times I hear young
Laughter
 and laugh myself.

I am old and the older I get the
Younger they seem

... the closer they
Watch me,
the narrower I become to them.

Old Elaine

Elaine refused to die in bed.
She deserved to sit in a chair
And die, she said. She ordered
Her son to tidy up the wicker
Wardrobe keeper and the hickory
Pair of chairs and air everything out
Best he could and fast, too, because
She'd fade into heaven by noon.

She told him to put the cookie jar
In the casket. He asked which one
And she answered weakly, the heart-
Shaped one.

Suddenly her son stood up, sliding
The aired-out chair her way saying
If she wanted his opinion it was odd
To die seated. Too rebellious. Too
Morbid for the rest of us, he said, to
Stare at your unsuitable sad-looking
Hickory seat. Be brave, old Elaine,
And die lying down.

Suntanned Laborers

Call everything by its name
And it will answer. Drive
Everything with a whip and
It will ache. Carve the pillars
Into laws, paw at the people,
Force the soul to the surface,
Urge the suntanned laborers
to sweat down their necks.

Bitter and undulating the boss-man
Avoids the mirrors and continues
To command an audience of work-drunk
Men who feed their families for pennies.
They sweat and sway the long hours until
The sun slips behind the mountain.

The Descent

Husky and handsome, the husband of her dreams.
Easy to please – hot meals and starched collars.
In winter, he chopped wood, sustaining fire's glow.

Singing in the church choir kept him humble but
romantic. La, La, La, he would test his voice in the
shower, every octave crisper and clearer.

Still newlyweds, they sat closely on a bench, feeling the
love-spark in their joined thighs. Casseroles and apple
pies predicted their future.

In time, he would abandon the choir and stay out
All night. Her meals would not satisfy him.

Pelt And Crumble

The rain pelted the bricks as if it
could cause them to crumble
but the mortar held. The rain
slammed the west-facing wood
until nails popped. The ejected
planks flew in the air like fence
pieces floating to the sky.

Gray with rain, the night
swirled in on itself like a
blanket being folded in fours.

The wind kicked and twisted
which hurled tools and pails
in every direction, even upward.

The only folks passing by in the
downpour wore slickers, slanting
their bodies forward.

Sly Boys Gliding

Children skid down the street
with arms out to the sides, riding
the wind, curving into the alley
where cats hide behind dumpsters
and run into view, scurrying up the fire-escape stairs.

Every day after school three sly boys pretend
                To be planes gliding in and out
                              of common streets with ease.

Honking sounds of the city compiled with the
shouts from mothers to sons
to come inside for dinner, go unanswered.

None of the children
                      listen until the third call is
accompanied by a voice so angry it trembles and
                      bites off pieces
of stinging words
and they worry their planes will crash if
they disobey.

Struggling Stardom

Vastly unpopular, the song made its debut,
High pitched and substantially shrill –
In a fit of rage, she prepared to redo.

Her manager advised her against a snafu
But curled his fingers into her hair as if to kill
Vastly unpopular, the song made its debut,

It was only a matter of time for her to renew
An interest in the opera, with her fervent will –
In a fit of rage, she prepared to redo.

The ghastly nature of trying to be true
Combined with instincts but bereft of skill…
Vastly unpopular, the song made its debut.

Thousands of fans were outraged but wooed,
Their simplicity unable to hold its fill…
In a fit of rage, she prepared to redo.

Not to be envious of the way she'd been shooed
She snuck behind the stage curtains, standing still –
Vastly unpopular, the song made its debut;
In a fit of rage, she prepared to redo.

Plain Truth

There's never been a way to get around a fact
Because the truth sticks to the pan it was cooked in.
People are plain until the truth returns to them –
Then they become simple.

I never lectured my boy about the right road to take.
The way I am it wouldn't take. He'll be the man I
Never was. He'll drive the cattle where I couldn't.
It'll be my boy who'll win the sheep race.

And when I'm grave-deep in my dug-down death,
It'll be my boy rubbing sticks together to show his
Boy the way to make a man's campfire.

A Stroll In The Dark

Thick slices of nighttime air poke
her nose until she inhales and sighs,
the deep kind of sigh that predicts
life is on a wicked path.

The farther she plods, the tenderer
She feels to let a cooing owl haunt
Her and a wolf howl startle her and
A growl from a distant animal cause
Her to wrap her shawl tighter at the
Shoulders.

She owns companies and manages
People in the heart of the city. Night
Is but an employee, she tells herself –
Whip it into shape, she tells herself.

As if shrugging off a coat, the purple night
Slips into blackness, revealing a delicate
Gray shroud that she must walk through.

Deep among the trees the woman stops...
Creating a stillness that matches the natural
Pace of the outdoors. She moans to declare
Her presence. Moaning is her elopement with
The free-spirited animals hiding in the shadows.
They understand why she's come.

Blizzard Then

Blizzard time, blizzard now, stand
Clear before it fluffs down. Snow descends
Gently at first. Obliterate the ugly with
The lovely – a fresh coat of new – an ability
To locate within itself the glitter and the
Twinkle of intricately-blueprinted snowflakes.

Blizzard time, blizzard now, with gravity
It piles curbside and creeps onto mailbox
Tops, lining driveways with white fur coats,
Sagging tree limbs with thick white cords of
Natural, glistening ice crystals.

Blizzard time, blizzard now, the cool air
Dusts the snow to one side and people
Bundled in their coats appear with shovels,
organizing their thoughts in a trance.

Falling snow brings amnesia and a hollow
But sweet feeling: The shovelers forget their
Lives to gaze on the transformative beauty of the
Snow going on for miles in front of their eyes.

Sun-Blotted Plainswoman

Presumption winced and gall defiled anew
A graphic portrait spared the crease of zest –
The jaunt, the jezebel, behold thy skew
And schism – sow thy mission sorceress.

Oh! Screech and thunderbolt, thy stark and graced
Protector perches beside the dove. The set,
Unsoiled bosom flirts but is not chaste
For holy splurge of sauce and demon let.

So laced and ankled, foot the path up grown
By serendipity, with children's hood
To cape the years and blanket that which is unknown
Among the trees and hills, the leaf and wood.

Aloof, saffron embers chant the moon –
They pounce, prevail some sinful sow of June.

Acknowledgements

"Hailing a Taxi", and "First Date" appeared in *Nixes Mate Review*, Summer 2017

"Chasm", "Cross the Wood So", "The Primordial Watch", "A&B", and "Ode to Down Below" all appeared in *Adelaide Literary Magazine* No. 8 July 2017

About the Author

Lisa Brognano is the author of a romance novel, *A Man for Prue* (Resplendence, 2017). Her poetry has appeared in both national and international literary journals. She holds two master's degrees, one in English and one in Art. Currently, she lives in New York with her husband.

Nixes Mate Books features small-batch artisanal literature, created by writers that use all 26 letters of the alphabet and then some, honing their craft the time-honored way: one line at a time.

More Nixes Mate titles:
ON BROAD SOUND | Rusty Barnes
KINKY KEEPS THE HOUSE CLEAN | Mari Deweese
SQUALL LINE ON THE HORIZON | Pris Campbell
COMES TO THIS | Jeff Weddle
HITCHHIKING BEATITUDES | Michael McInnis
AIR & OTHER STORIES | Lauren Leja
WAITING FOR AN ANSWER | Heather Sullivan
A WORLD WHERE | Paul Brookes
MY SOUTHERN CHILDHOOD | Pris Campbell
THE PAUL BUNYAN BALLROOM | Bud Backen

Forthcoming titles from Nixes Mate:
NIXES MATE REVIEW ANTHOLOGY 2016/17
CAPP ROAD | Matt Borczon
LUBBOCK ELECTRIC | Anne Elezabeth Pluto
STARLAND | Jessica Purdy
HEART OF THE BROKEN WORLD | Jeff Weddle
JESUS IN THE GHOST ROOM | Rusty Barnes
SMOKEY OF THE MIGRAINES | Michael McInnis

nixesmate.pub/books

www.ingramcontent.com/pod-product-compliance
Lightning Source LLC
Chambersburg PA
CBHW052135010526
44113CB00036B/2272